A HAT

by Lynn Trepicchio

illustrated by Vicky Bolling

Harcourt

Orlando   Boston   Dallas   Chicago   San Diego

Visit *The Learning Site!*

www.harcourtschool.com

Sam ran up.

Sam ran down.

Sam ran up.

Sam ran down.

Sam ran up.

Sam ran down.

Sam ran to a hat.